Joy Richardson

Gareth Stevens Publishing
MILWAUKEE

For a free color catalog describing Gareth Stevens' list of high-quality books and multimedia programs, call 1-800-542-2595 (USA) or 1-800-461-9120 (Canada). Gareth Stevens Publishing's Fax: (414) 225-0377.

Gareth Stevens Publishing would like to thank Gundega Spons of the Milwaukee Art Museum for her kind and professional help with the information in this book.

Library of Congress Cataloging-in-Publication Data available upon request from publisher. Fax (414) 225-0377 for the attention of the Publishing Records Department.

ISBN 0-8368-2628-0

This North American edition first published in 2000 by
Gareth Stevens Publishing
1555 North RiverCenter Drive, Suite 201
Milwaukee, Wisconsin 53212 USA

Original edition © 1998 by Franklin Watts. First published in 1998 as *Telling a Story* by Franklin Watts, 96 Leonard Street, London, EC2A 4RH, United Kingdom. This U.S. edition © 2000 by Gareth Stevens, Inc. Additional end matter © 2000 by Gareth Stevens, Inc.

Gareth Stevens Editor: Monica Rausch
Gareth Stevens Cover Designer: Joel Bucaro
U.K. Editor: Sarah Ridley
U.K. Art Director: Robert Walster
U.K. Designer: White Design

Photographs: © Bodleian Library, Oxford, pp. 20-21; © Trustees of the British Museum, London, pp. 4-5; © Christie's Images/Bridgeman Art Library, pp. 16-17, 26 (detail); © Musées Royaux des Beaux Arts de Belgique, Brussels/Bridgeman Art Library, pp. 12-13, 29; National Gallery, London, pp. 6-7, 8-9, 18-19, 28 (detail), 30, 31; National Galleries of Scotland, cover, pp. 22-23, 24-25, 28 (detail); by courtesy of the National Portrait Gallery, London, pp. 14-15, 27; © RMN/Musée du Petit Palais pp. 10-11, 26 (detail).

Printed in Mexico

1 2 3 4 5 6 7 8 9 04 03 02 01 00

Contents

For additional information about the artists and paintings, see pages 30-31.

A Scene from the
Book of the Dead of Anhai

painted by an Egyptian artist

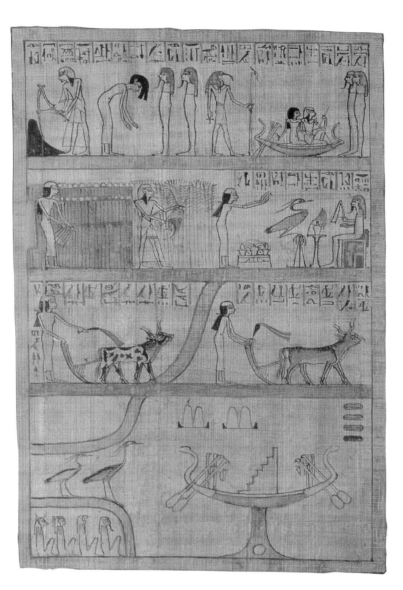

This painting was placed in a tomb. The story
it tells is part of a guide to the land of the dead.

The Legend of the Wolf of Gubbio
painted by Stefano di Giovanni Sassetta

Saint Francis and the wolf make a deal. In return for food, the wolf will stop attacking people.

*A boat sails on
the Nile River.*

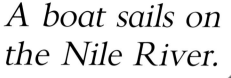

*Reeds grow
tall and are
ready for
cutting.*

*Oxen plow
the land.*

The Legend of the Wolf of Gubbio
painted by Stefano di Giovanni Sassetta

Saint Francis and the wolf make a deal. In return for food, the wolf will stop attacking people.

A boat sails on
the Nile River.

Reeds grow
tall and are
ready for
cutting.

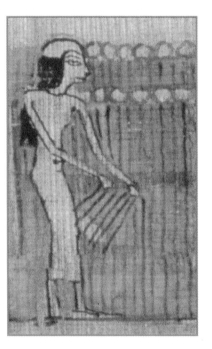

Oxen plow
the land.

They shake hands
on the agreement.

A lawyer writes
everything down.

Look at what the
wolf has done.

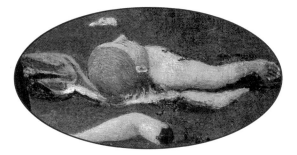

No wonder people
were frightened.

Saint George and the Dragon
painted by Paolo Uccello

Saint George rescues a princess
from the hungry dragon.

The horse rears.

Saint George strikes with his lance.

The dragon meets his match.

The princess looks on.

Theseus and the Minotaur

painted by the Master of the
Campana Cassoni

Theseus sails across the sea to
kill the minotaur in the maze. Ariadne
gives him thread to mark his route.

How many times does Theseus appear in the painting?

Ariadne waits for him to return.

Theseus kills the minotaur.

Theseus and his friends sail safely away.

Landscape with the Fall of Icarus
painted by Pieter Bruegel

Icarus tried to fly like a bird, but the sun
melted the wax that held his wings together.

Icarus plunges into the sea.

Sheep graze quietly beside the shepherd and his dog.

Ships sail on their way.

Does anyone notice Icarus falling out of the sky?

Sir Henry Unton (detail)
painted by an unknown artist

Follow the story of one man's life,
from his birth to his death.

Find him in his mother's arms,

studying at a university,

traveling,

playing music,

feasting at home,

becoming ill,

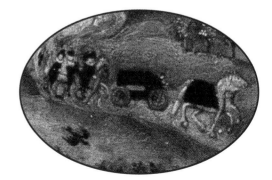

and at his funeral.

The Animals Entering the Ark

painted by Jacob II Savery

Noah boarded animals in pairs on his boat
to save them from the coming flood.

Birds fly around as storm clouds gather.

Animals board the ark.

Can you find a mate for these creatures?

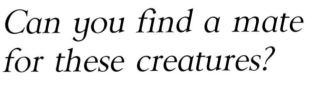

Belshazzar's Feast
painted by Rembrandt

What is that strange writing? Everyone stops to stare at the mysterious marks on the wall.

A hand appears out of nowhere.

The King's eyes
nearly pop out
of his head.

Wine spills.

Frightened faces
gape at the sight.

An Episode from
The Thousand and One Nights

painted by a Mughal artist

A prince traveled the world to
find the magical princess.

Upon finding her, the happy prince and princess fly away together.

Friendly demons carry them along.

Winged servants float through the air in cloud carriages.

The earth below bursts into life.

The Quarrel of Oberon and Titania

painted by Sir Joseph Noel Paton

On a magical midsummer's night, the King and Queen of the fairies argue over a little boy.

Fairies flutter
through the forest.

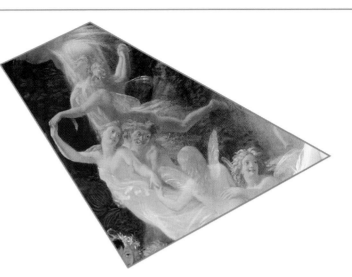

The boy clings
to Titania.

Oberon wants
to take the
boy away.

Puck will
help the King.

The Pied Piper of Hamelin
painted by James Elder Christie

The Pied Piper plays his magic pipe.
Children follow him and are never seen again.

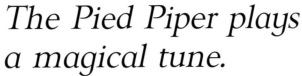

The tune makes
children happy.

The children
follow him
through the
woods.

Even a baby is
brought along.

25

Storytelling with Paint

Choosing a story

Artists often choose just a small part of a story to paint.

Try painting a small part of one of the stories in this book.

From start to finish

Some paintings show several parts of a story all rolled into one.

Try combining two parts of the same story to make one painting.

For help, look at pages 4, 10, and 14.

Life story

Think of five important events in your own life.

Try putting them all into a single painting that tells the story of your life so far.

For help, look at pages 4 and 14.

Stories within stories

Artists often add other, smaller scenes to their paintings.

Try telling your own story about these little scenes.

For help, look at pages 6, 12, and 22.

Story focus

A picture may lead your eye straight to the main character or event,
or you may have to look closely to find it.

Try painting this story with the main event going on in the foreground.

For help, look at pages 10 and 12.

More about the paintings in this book

■ A Scene from the Book of the Dead of Anhai *(page 4)*

These scenes were painted on papyrus in ancient Egypt around 1150 B.C. They come from a Book of the Dead that was placed in a tomb as a guide to the afterlife. The scenes show the dead man cultivating the land in the Field of Reeds, a home away from home in paradise where the dead were believed to dwell. Such scenes were created to help link the pleasant life of ancient Egypt with the afterlife.

■ The Legend of the Wolf of Gubbio *(page 6)*

Stefano di Giovanni Sassetta (about 1392-1450) was an Italian painter who worked in Siena. This painting was created for the altar of a church. It was one of eight small panels showing scenes from the life of Saint Francis, a peacemaker who had a special way with animals.

■ Saint George and the Dragon *(page 8)*

Paolo Uccello (1397-1475) lived in Florence, Italy. In this painting, he shows the legend of Saint George rescuing the king's daughter, who had been chosen as the flesh-eating dragon's latest victim. Uccello shows Saint George riding to the rescue, and he also shows the next part of the story, when the princess is already calmly holding the subdued dragon by a lead.

■ Theseus and the Minotaur *(page 10)*

The Master of the Campana Cassoni (whose real name is unknown) made this painting around 1510. The painting shows the ancient Greek legend of Theseus killing the minotaur in a modern Italian setting. It also shows the entire sequence of the story.

■ Landscape with the Fall of Icarus *(page 12)*

Pieter Bruegel the Elder (about 1525-1569) was a Dutch painter. Daedalus and his son Icarus escaped from Crete on wings that were made from feathers and attached to the body with wax. Icarus flew too close to the sun, causing the wax to melt, and the wings fell apart. Bruegel shows life going on as usual, as Icarus disappears into the sea.

■ Sir Henry Unton *(page 14)*

An unknown artist painted this picture around 1596. The main events of Unton's life are shown counterclockwise from the bottom right, and his life at home is illustrated in the middle. The story continues onto the left half of the painting (not shown here) with Unton's funeral and a portrait of him.

The Animals Entering the Ark *(page 16)*

Jacob II Savery (1593-1627) was a Dutch painter. This picture tells the story of Noah's Ark from the book of Genesis in the Bible. God told Noah to build a giant boat so that when the coming rain flooded the earth, his family and two animals of each species would be saved.

Belshazzar's Feast *(page 18)*

Rembrandt (1606-1669) was a Dutch painter. Here he captures a dramatic moment from a Bible story. Writing appeared mysteriously on the wall, interrupting King Belshazzar's feast. Only Daniel, a Jewish servant, could read what it said: the King, who had taken gold and silver from the temple in Jerusalem, was to be punished. Enemies attacked that night, and King Belshazzar died.

An Episode from *The Thousand and One Nights* *(page 20)*

This painting was done around 1760 by a Mughal artist. It illustrates the amazing tale of the Egyptian Prince Saif ul-Muluk, who had many adventures in his quest for Badi'al-Jamal. She was a princess of the Jinn, superhuman beings who appear in many forms. The story comes from the great Arabic collection *The Thousand and One Nights*.

The Quarrel of Oberon and Titania *(page 22)*

Sir Joseph Noel Paton (1821-1901) lived in Scotland. This picture illustrates a scene from William Shakespeare's play *A Midsummer Night's Dream*. Puck helps make magic so that Titania falls in love with whomever she first sees on waking. The forest is full of fairy creatures on this most magical night of the year.

The Pied Piper of Hamelin *(page 24)*

James Elder Christie (1847-1914) was a Scottish painter. "The Pied Piper of Hamelin" is a German legend from the thirteenth century. The Pied Piper rid Hamelin of a plague of rats. When he was not paid for this service, he played his magic pipe again. All the children followed him out of the city and never returned.

Glossary

board (v): to go onto a ship or plane.

demons: mean or evil spirits.

episode: a scene or part of a longer story.

foreground: the part of a picture that seems to be the closest to the viewer.

gape: to stare at with an open mouth.

lance: a long sword, often used by armored knights for jousting.

legend: a story handed down over time. The story may or may not be true, but is often believed by many people.

maze: a network of paths leading from one place to another and in which there are many dead ends, making it difficult to find an exit or entrance.

minotaur: a beast that is half man, half bull.

quarrel: argue; fight.

route: a path leading from one place to another.

subdued: to be under control; defeated.

tomb: a vault for the dead.

Web Sites

Kinder Art Art Education
www.kinderart.com/lessons.htm

Lunaland Online Story Site
www.lunaland.co.za

Due to the dynamic nature of the Internet, some web sites stay current longer than others. To find additional web sites, use a reliable search engine with one or more of the following keywords: *art, legends, A Midsummer Night's Dream, painting, Rembrandt,* and *storytelling.*

Index